T0068979

The dust of just beginning

The dust of just beginning

Don kerr

AU PRESS

2010 Don Kerr

Published by AU Press, Athabasca University
1200, 10011 – 109 Street
Edmonton, AB T5J 3S8

Library and Archives Canada Cataloguing in Publication

Kerr, Don
The dust of just beginning / Don Kerr.

(Mingling voices, ISSN 1917-9405)
Poems.
Issued also in an electronic format (978-1-897425-93-0).
ISBN 978-1-897425-92-3

I. Title.
II. Series: Mingling voices

PS8571.E71D88 2010   C811'.54   C2010-904774-5

Cover and book design by Natalie Olsen, Kisscut Design.
Cover image by Don Proch, *Asessippi Valley* (2006).
Author photo by Hans Dommasch.
Printed and bound in Canada by Marquis Book Printing.

This publication is licensed under a Creative Commons
License, Attribution-Noncommercial-No Derivative
Works 2.5 Canada: see www.creativecommons.org. The
text may be reproduced for non-commercial purposes,
provided that credit is given to the original author.

To obtain permission for uses beyond those outlined in
the Creative Commons license, please contact AU Press,
Athabasca University, at aupress@athabascau.ca.

A volume in the Mingling Voices series:
ISSN 1917-9405 (Print)   ISSN 1917-9413 (Online)

JUST BEGINNING

FOR IT'S LOVE

JOURNEY MAN

contents

we are the echo

to escape onto paper

JUST
BEGINNING

a height of prairies

a height of prairies over the river
sideways sun in the brown
stubble, twisted speech
of dead trees, the duplicitous
sun, but in decline, eyes
seeing for miles, all
at the same moment, elsewhere
the room with the blinds drawn,
the cancer advancing like traffic

or the smell in the corridor
of cooking, a fire hose for decor,
a life, long at its time, unmet
in words, a day in the
Shirley apartments, the smell
of cooking, long demolished,
home to a bowling alley,
automobile garage, passing
unmarked

a day in Connaught
in Ladbroke Road

Billy

look, Billy dead, the city empties,
the city of London empties,
if we don't enter we needn't
remember, nor see others
in his room, his things
scattered, his ghost thin
in my belly   what is there to say
without the listening man?

your death Billy,
confounding time, burying
your friends, burying the stories,
plentiful as books in your room,
your Vancouver, long buried,
long demolished, sun the liar
saying this is the last of all days, yet
we bound for the next day, your music
on the tape deck, we travel
two ways now, playing you
one day at a time

Billy at Notting Hill
at Ladbroke Road
at Gennaro's, at Prost's,
talking the eyes out of a girl,
dancing near the wide Saskatchewan
in shoes shiny enough to show
the mossy face, Billy leaving
Christmas at Finchley for the
eight-mile walk or crying
in the crowded hospital at Paddington
and saying I don't usually cry,
the pain swallowing Billy

the lady gardener, Anne Szum

the night edges over the house
into the branches of the tree
the branches of the dark green fir
into the forest of the peony
into the dirt under the peony

in the dead centre of the day
in the mid of the mid day
the sun like a perennial
the bluebells happy in the
sweet breeze the lilies
pointing skyward the raspberries
in spiky bud all wait oh they all wait
for their first love the lady
gardener but she is unavoidably
detained the faces of the pansies
the petunias watch and wait but
she is unavoidably
detained

the voice of Anne

if your words fall into her ear
and you are in the same room
the one with the column of cds
the heater that eats logs
the walls insulated with books of poetry

in that room, your words falling
into that ear, need no other home
until she, the lady gardener,
dwells only in our rooms
cluttered as they are
with all matter of the living
absently watching cars
people and the faintest
of faint snow falling
from a heaven grey as ghosts
or your eccentric angels falling
into the pie-shaped lot
on Connaught saying in their
odd way for heaven's sake
pick the raspberries
red as thick blood
the sparrow hopping about
looking for the ear to pour
its song into while I, bereft,
fall back into the habit of books

and she sits, makes tea,
tends the garden, reads,
in the voice of Anne,
all days in disarray

sun

if there is no sun
and the sky draws down
you walk through
a veil of mist and are not
at home

sun shone before you knew
sun and wherever you travel sun
is your home your dream
of Rome   sun rising
and falling in Claude
of Lorraine   the wide bay
or the bones leaning like flames
into only sun

when you see sun
rocking the lake, firing the woods
with a latticework that greens
the ferns, laying great hands
on the hills, scouring the bare
valleys and the small forests
of your arms and legs,
would you praise god?
or let the mind go dead,
the body drowsy   bathing
in sun heat and day light

the jesus poems

jesus held me
in the grip of hell
my grade three teacher
lit the fire
and only prayer
said over and over and over
might keep me green and cool
terrified always to re-enter
the brick prison of St. Joe's School
or to tell the terror
held me in thrall

baseball was the way
and the light of day
jesus never played baseball
maybe umpire or scorekeeper
but the soft bunt down third
the leaping catch at second
to be lead-off batter
to wait in the on-deck circle
to do the chatter
to win at tough
St. Mary's to forget the fire
concentrating on the next pitch
was the best way out of
all that other stuff

2.

There is nothing I believe
with mathematical precision,
no equation out of the self.
If lonely enough or vanishing enough
would Odetta effect a cure?
Patsy Cline or *Casablanca?*
Yet there is the temptation,
the nothing into everything,
true life in death, the miracle
of the cross, the Catholic
calculating machine.

easy enough to say
black on a health day

sweet church, its large
emptiness, candles burning
for the dead, the boy counting
how many souls could fit and fly
in the large auditorium of god,
quits at thousands, looks
at silence, the creak of a kneeler
echoes, he kneeling, hands clasped
holy, sinks his teeth into the
varnished pew to leave his mark,
under St. Joseph in the brown
cloak with a staff the candles
burning like souls, like hell,
like purgatory and so beautiful,
eyes caught, body gone quiet
he crosses himself,
walks down the stone steps
into the wide street

4.

this was the sermon
that a great garden
our heart's desire
green and golden
was surrounded by a high fence
with a narrow entrance
and outside all was fury and fire
storm and stormy plains
the land of all fear

I knew I would never
discover that narrow way
to the green garden
and day after day
I picked the deadhead poppies
in my mom's garden that they
would flower orange and yellow
like fire all the days
of summer

5.

Is it possible to be a fallen away
United Churcher? Like my dad.
We discovered in the apple-box
bookshelves in the basement his prize
for bible studies in grade six
in Nokomis. That wasn't
the father we knew. He attended
Catholic mass with my mother
on Easter Sunday and was reading
a detective novel in the back pew
when the priest, confessions over,
asked him if it was the good book.
My dad, halfway through
a Rex Stout, grinned. He was
an accountant but not
a Catholic. His balance sheet
was numerical. "Who made you?"
"God made me to …" After church
wind in trees makes shadows.

6.

What was it you called me?
catholic or socialist.
Call me something less
something you know little of.
Call me baroque.
Fellini says labels
should go on suitcases.

The old house on eleventh
with so many gimcracks
on the lawn folks could not
fathom the lady maker, mad
they said, their clothes
shrinking. Or a church
I saw as a kid, basement
only, or the one tree left
where we necked in the shadow
of long-gone Rosary Hall we edging
nearer to finale but hanging
fire   anteroom to living room
and if you talk

        don't focus

           okay

7.

for fear, I moved silently
for fear, I said little
for fear, I kept to myself
for fear, on my knees in prayer
for fear, never entering
for fear, never entering
for fear, no life but fear

the body poems

1.

the body is sick
the head says
the body is growing
mosquito bites
ankle aches belly boils
and the like
just to spite mind
no choice but to live above that damn body
head whose clarity reviles
the accident of body
wants to be left alone
feels trapped in
errant & bloody sullied
stink of flesh and bone

2.

nearing the end, the body failing,
you learn modesty in all desires,
except the desire for desire,
a modest thirst, the rose hip
or the lemon or the mint tea,
settling inoffensively in that body

oh that was

in its time so arrogant,
so easy in its words
a soft-shoe body
dancing body
blues body

ahh

3.

when I feel awful, so far at least,
it's provisional, like a hangover
that has always its slow end
encoded in the very libations
you drank, and at this moment
on a cool morning in October
the fumes from my coffee
pour over this page like
clouds in fast motion, so
light a grey, so tentative,
so provisional

4.

the worm under the skin
leaches colour, rolling
in the sun, basking in dark,
the colour of cement, pocked,
scarred with cracks, worn,
walked on, the day on the move,
cars talking in their boring way,
the sun blueing the sky, the worm
grinning over its first coffee of the day

5. a modest carnality

when I ordered a grande au lait
on Denman the girl asked,
two or three shots of espresso
and I said two, I wasn't man
enough for three and she said
she was, the modest carnality,
in the swing-walk of the waitress,
in the hug of greeting, in the
amazing summer legs of the
server girl, in this
light touch and that,
in the communion of smiles,
the perfect stranger, the
touch on the shoulder, the purring
of invisible antennae,
in for a penny

6. the dance

those times ago   the dance
enveloping us none other
than dance   hip check
eye trap   sun
rising in a series of steps
down the railroad hotel
body wakes in the shank
of next afternoon   the sun
imprinting itself in the brain
find a beer   start a
slow dance waiting
for the music of your lover
to take you over
and over again

the waters of life

which then are the waters of life?
at Fishing Lake on quiet days
the water lolling about
like a lazy fish

at Windermere the bonfire
of evening at the end
of the lapping day

at English Bay the eye
drawn to the line
where water ends
and sky begins

waves washing ashore
under the still water sky

what then is free?

like water to find your own level
without guilt
to fade from view
while others talk
to arrive at each day
without a plan but with,
let us say, poems to write
in the sun of morning
to have an appointment for lunch
you want to keep

the rote beads

He knew he should be bereft
at the prayers for his mother
it was what he felt but
when the old priest did
the stations of the rosary
the rote beads he felt
only anger. His mother
had said the trouble
with the Catholic seniors
residence was everybody
was so damned religious.
Age eating at her
never got all the way.

the last day

he forgot one wound
in another
one ghastly presence
replaced by another
a kind of motion disease
from body part to body
part, head to belly to
limb, this day the last day
of the freshly dead
hearing all the words
that lay you under
on the last ride
the cars smelling each other
down memorial drive
under the elm roof
shredding the sun

then the day too is done

I told you I could drive

I've become a brandy drinker
a swirl at the bottom of the fat-bellied
glass, with the elegant scent

on a particular day
of no particular sort
my mother, having received
her first driver's licence,
aged 72, drove to my father's grave
and said, "See, Cam, I told you I could drive,"
used one tank of gas and sold us the car

it's not a bad brandy
I should be drinking
rye and ginger
my father's and his brother's
and Canada's national drink

a toast to our fallen comrades

Ila

Ila who tended
our kids with verve,
leaving us now behind
the wind beating us
down swallowing all
testimonials, chilling us
to the bone, driving us
to the warm cars,
you betcha,
Ila in the cold, cold
ground, brother took the soil
temperature, four inches
down it was only thirty
can't plant, yep, clouds
bundling over the April grey
stubble, cars gone, you
betcha

a memory

a memory
rattling in the head
the face of one long
dead in the dream
in the city you've never been
the ambulance in its white coat
its cargo dying
in the dead of winter

the ghost in the belly

song by Mabel Mercer
by Oscar Brown
by Nina Simone
is then and then

oh then

oh then

while journeys end
they begin again
all finales provisional
the meeting over   the walking begins
the walking over the bus begins   it's
hardly news   years ago there was
one sunset I decided would never
end   colours blurring   the evening
by the river   whatever evening
it was   remains still   colours blurring
all going down and every
sundown is a replay
of that evening   antennae
quivering

oh then

gone large gone small

is it rooms or parks
we desire wombs or space
low roofs or sky high
the friend in the room
at Ladbroke has died
the room at Connaught
the room where the stories
were stored gone dark
the city empties
street by street
gone large gone small

the dust of just beginning

the trees by the river yellowing
the day without breeze
golden coins hovering
in the blue sun
the car tailing through
parkland or prairie
a chill in the air
first taste of winter
white and cold
is the taste of the first melt
on the south side of stores
on Broadway where the low rise
encourages spring arriving
street by street everywhere
the scent of dust
slow stepping spring
in the nostril
the dust of just
beginning

for it's love

love poems

for it's love owns the body
makes it bend like a tree
in the wind all one way

for it's love owns the heart
makes it drown in the flood
in the wild tide of love

for it's love owns the head
eyes look where they will
there are no thoughts but love

the day going on forever
all parts caught by love
nowhere to turn but love

2. remembrance of love

remembrance of love
the internal collapse as you
walked in the door in any
room at all   in church
the icon my eyes
prayed to   oh then
heart full   heart sick
there outside my self
my self was standing

a sweater of let us say pink
where breasts like birds
in nests entered my nervous
system and I was a goner

half in love with loss

3. music in the veins

music in the veins
feet a life of their own
it was nina simone
oh flo flo flo me la and on
the move till dawn
the partner at arm's length
or close enough to trade
body parts all the way down
the mind on half pay
waiting for nina to say
it was time to flo me la
in our juice-laden bodies

and who among us in the tall café
has swallowed a ghost today

4. the nameless heart

the nameless heart
named heart drowns under
the flood and reaches for dry
land receding faster than grasp

the heart in deep water
pumping for all it's worth
its aorta and its long
tentacles like a winter
elm tree is desperate
for the sign
for the saving grace
for the word from you oh lady
day to save this nameless
heart of mine

love can be
so muted a solo
so sweet a duet
daily the jazz trio
in the late-night lounge
the talking going on
at the low tables
round as wafers
at odd times the bar
gone quiet   the piano
so fluent in the night
or driving for miles
on the ease of the wide
four-lane highway joining
the rv park on full hookup
for the night

mall

in the mall the family of man
has gone forth and multiplied
and the cars of the family of man
have gone forth and multiplied
busy days in the
fabricated world

enough of waiting, yes,
the buying, selling, the walking
and waiting, cars in their carspots,
the endless lines of desires,
the feet dying, the sulking,
the slow fire of anger,
trying to stay sane,
the sun on high and where
is a stranger to start
the whole stupid bloody thing
all over again

body poems II, the black poet

1. narcissus

translation is hard
walking is easy

love is a long line
and kissing is shorthand

it's a sweet thing to say
I wrote poetry in Spain
I wish I could say that

black is the colour
of my true love's heart

in the magic room
we slept well
you went bloody wild,
Narcissus,
bloody wild,
you said
proud as hell

2. kill speak

kill speak, she said,
kill speak and take me to bed
oh I'm too timid, I said,
too timid to take you to bed

life, she said, is so bloody bad
I had a devil for a dad
I'm too timid I said,
too timid to take you to bed

I've a body a devil can love
a body ripe for that guy up above
I've a mind that believes in God
and a body that tries to be good

I've two breasts and a hungry cunt
come aboard and join in the hunt
sweet Lord protect me I ask you please
sweet Lord before I fall to my knees

kill speak me baby, she said,
kill speak and take me to bed
I never learned kill speak, he said,
shall I kill self to enter your bed?

yes, she said, yes
well, he said, hmm

3. love is the knife

love is the knife
that cuts to the bone
oh a fine knife
an old lacerator
plunged into ugly love,
she said, as if saying it
made it more

4. fantasies

the fantasies
gorge themselves on the barren
bed   fantasy populates
                              every which way
while plain day is a
                              windy blue
the first red finger of tulip
in the smelly mulch reborning
in the wrinkled leaves

first splash

5. the ease of wit

remember the days
of the ease of wit
the flowing in and out
focus the faux pas,
surface in lieu
of the dead serious,
the art of the interrupt
death to tirade but
all honour to the solo
as for love give cole
porter the last aperçu

journey man

a fearful carnality

today the clouds are aesthetic
white & thin, elegant &
optimistic   yet dissolve
into sun in a fearful
carnality   you walking or
driving under them as if you
were important   your eyes
gorged   the sun in that high-lit
scam dressing you down
lashing you to the day
sun-lashed back   forty lashes
if you please to bring the
dead to light
billy & anne   kitty & cam
the light so thick
by midday death
was in decay

lost and found

lost on this road
we know like the back of our hand
under clouds that cannot hold still
can hold no shape at all
of course we are expected
the scotch waiting in the cupboard hall
but nobody knows where we are
on the highway like any other
in the car that's any car
on some wave or other on our way
to the old port of call

my road

this is my road
no one else wants it
the clouds over my road
are first-rate clouds
the fields by my road
are Olympic-sized fields
and I'm on the old way
to discover the exact feeling
of driving in the sweet spring
on the great plains
the road free of language
the signs sparse
life thin
cars fast

the high sun
in passing gear
on my road

that runs and
runs

the first day

In the beginning there was delay
In the beginning rain was already falling
In the beginning the cell phone worked overtime
In the beginning the last wash was done
the last flowers planted
In the beginning the travelling bags
overflowed with anticipation
and the dog left home in the company of a girl
worth wagging her tail over
In the beginning the house resumed its silence
In the beginning the van groaned
the baby pushed all the buttons
and the clock quit
In the beginning the rain clouds came in layers
already in the coastal weather
we were travelling to
In the beginning the fields stretched forever
and the kids played pick-a-number
In the beginning the black highway
drew us onward
In the beginning we were our destination

In the middle a patch of blue sky appeared
We were all reassured
In the middle he saw the past
the Scamp the Dart the Rambler the Chevrolet
His eyes were the same
They saw what was there
The highways were wider smoother
In the middle the van
does not break down
in the rubber-tire world
In the middle he thought
of whiskey at the terminus
He thought no further ahead than that
In the middle the kids
ran round the park in Vegreville
and invented happiness
In the middle the sun came out
He was sunloving and mindnumb
now time the only time
just like last time
In the middle the sun
rambled all over the place

and they sang Blue Skies
In the middle the baby yelled "cows cows"
and became the cowboy
In the middle he wanted that other time
He wanted that other time
the blue Chevrolet just before
death entered the world
Oh he wanted that other time
Today he wanted today
already lonely for today
and our vanguard group of seven
in the beginning the middle and the end

In the end they made four correct turns
In the end they sat on the deck
in the full sun
Now only the earth moved
In the end the barbecue worked on their behalf
In the end they drove for more beer
The evening was long at the end of June
In the end the clouds massed, ran, thinned,
grew ramparts, washboards, were white,
were grey, were yellow with sundown,
streaked with lightning, poured rain
In the end the cards appeared
In the end the television captured the children
In the end our eyes collapsed and we dreamt
travelling invisible roads
At the end of the first day

where are we going next year?

bad highway out of Richdale
makes Saskatchewan drivers
feel right at home

the Hanna escarpment says
the days of the prairie
are numbered
the valley of the Red Deer
is at hand
clouds in our heaven cool
with mountain air
we surround our old friend
on two sides
and we are where we
were meant to be

Graham, give me my pillow.
It's a chicken.
Give me my chicken.
It's a turkey.
Graham!
You have to pay fifteen, thirty,
eighty thousand dollars.
Booger brain.
You're a barney.
You're a guinea pig.
I'm hungry.
Where are we going next year?

to the tax man

rolling down the railroad line
a mile-long container train
saving all that gasoline
spent on the four-lane highway
by trucks, cars, and us today
if I write enough to mean
we'll deduct the gasoline
don't need a regular metre
to deduct another litre
but hell if I write enough
I'll take the motel cost off
hey, hey, this land is our land
travelling on the tax man

journey man

I am a journey man
on the low road high road
the flags of the clouds
blowing upstream all a-flutter
my heart   the journey man
on the known roads
fresh this morning as
new-baked sun

you dream the poem

around the corner the perfect
valley
the farmhouse with a silver roof
burning
the easy highway the sun
on your leg

the highway is the narrative cutting through
the chaos of trees
five days on the road in your own
home
each highway a number each curve
nameless
to Kamloops or Cache Creek or the legendary
Yakk
going the speed limit plus
five
in a meeting in a basement room one window only
you dream the poem of car
and road

tough terrain

in the new town
on the wrong road
the women shopping
the sky lowering   a woman
with white breasts drives
off in a four-wheel the day
waiting for her on the edge
of age   let the story begin
the story of giving up
smoking or beating cancer
or the story of love which
carries her away like
a ferocious four-wheel
in tough terrain

mind riding

in the room and travelling too
you look me in the eye and
see nothing at all
this random mind riding
on highways of no man's devising
no man can map mind
which has itself forgotten
where it is   so wandering it is
so absent   as if all walls
were open road   the eye
closed shall go
where it will

Blue River

"You're so old
 you'll forget
 where you come from."
 Nope.
 I come from youth.
"You're so old
 you'll forget
 where you're going to."
 I'm going to Blue River
 by brown cows and green trees
 rock face and fast river.

we are THE echo

kelly's alley

he walked into the wrong alley
that was kelly's alley
daydreaming into danger
for the day of the bully
was at hand by the broken
garage that smelled of poop
eyes opening   legs like jelly
"you come back I'll break yr fuckin'
head" backing out in terror
end of the alley in sight   tremor
of hope

hunting rabbits

hunting rabbits with a .22
pulling the barbed wire apart
to crawl through
into the hilly bush
no crop no cow no farmhouse
eyes alive watching for
movement in the brush
bang, bang, got him!
got him! said Ted,
dead rabbit brown
dark blood stain
lying in the spiky grass
our eyes alive watching again
for movement in the low bush

on the line

to work the line
is to live in the mind
the body repeating itself
hand over hand over hand
the mind on weekend

to work the line
is to become the machine
feed it with bottles at one end
pack them out the other
at night grease the nipples
the bottle-washing machine
on general drone the labelling
machine on steady clunk clank
we the most quiet part of
the machine   each in his own
reverie of lawn or lake or love
all bodies equal
on the line

summer south

picking cherries in the Okanagan
tall pointed ladders lift you
to the long view, lake, hills,
roadway flowing with cars,
a kind of power to be so tall
in the cave of a tree, clouds
streaming over the brown hills,
you pause, for the moment, the work
on hold, of course it's summer,
summer south, obstreperously
summer, in a place you are
and aren't and you think
have I given god the slip
perched high in the tree
the purple cherries
bursting in the mouth

Cousin Lynda

in Vernon Cousin Lynda was on the hunt
for a hundred pounds of cucumbers
a hundred pounds of tomatoes
for dill pickles for relish
pick them herself at 45¢ a pound
to lay away the preserves
preserving herself   publishing
pickles   I said, you're
your mother and she said
yes

water boy

the body of the boy leaps
into deep water   dives
under the body of water
frog boy   water boy
danger boy   no fears   mother
a blur way up there   sound
echoes in the sweet
deep water

we are the echo

faces echo
skip a father or so
the nose of the clan ringrose
is on the rampage
or the black black hair
of the kerrs from god knows
where   all the old photos
unnamed   stiff with time
or I see in the bar
an echo of doug
dead a dozen years ago
because they were after him
the gamblers   paranoia   awful
as dog piss in the snow
the collie like the collie
who whelped her all in the face
the tail markings high and low
of the dead we are the echo

this is the day nothing happens
a meeting to say we've come to the end
of the agenda for today   soccer on tv
and hotspur won   this is the day
nothing happens   listening
for the first time to a cd
by mark   this is the day
nothing happens   a son says
how his interview went
excellent   a sister-in-law
had half a lung removed
and is under morphine
this is the day nothing happens
this is the day nothing happens
to you

body idling over

I bike to the coffee shop
sun stepping in the window
body idling over
art on the wall
music on the sound system
"Oh my, oh my, why must I explain?"
the dark tenor sings   girl
in a ball cap walks past
the coffee oasis
and there's that blue sky
burning and pine trees
tall as the school
newspapers to tell of the
parent trap   Cuba's secrets
poverty in Manila and then
I dream   body idling over
to be on the road at Hope
with all its intersections

to escape onto paper

into the woods

into the woods walked the man
dedicated to ecology, and he walked in
without a pen, I said, without a pen!
incredulous that joy should have no record,
as if the self would boil and bubble
unrecorded, all of life clammering
to escape onto paper

word off

she walks in and desolates
the day, a particular flavour
of face, a blonde face, greyish
hair, loose blue shirt,
pressed jeans, wordless,
slender as a knife, eyes
like weapons   me
working hard to word
her off

victim of story

Philoctetes remains true
to his pain, the festering
leg, for years abandoned
on the rocky island, and no
words of Odysseus the political,
no promise of fame, of victory,
they are but words to the pain
which is his, which is
who he has become, but myth
more strong than self
and the god from the machine
drove Philoctetes to Troy,
another victim of story

88 /

at the end of his fifth whiskey
he became certain he was certain
and those who spoke of the price
of gold of shares in Nortel of the
Cayman Islands as grand tax haven were
he was certain in his brilliant head
dead wrong and dead dead

the dead tired poem

on the day of the hangover
on the day of the hollow chest
on the day of the body in charge
on the day of the rapid cloud
on the day of the tossed trees
        in full bloom
on the day of the dead eye
body working to hold its head up
everyone else exuding health
like a plague of grin
a day on which the first beer
lay on the horizon
on the dead day of
the dead tired poem

the anonymous clouds

there is no centre on
a glum day   the anonymous clouds
over the river whose cross-hatched
waves cannot be named
one from another
or the weeds   the bush   the trees

sit on my bench for a minute
or by some other method
of measure   shadows moving
in the short-hair grass

never start from here

in the metropole
the weight of opinion

we live in a thin country
poets slip out sideways

traffic is heavy and art
brief   poem inert
lives in an unmarked
grave   never start
from here

Samuel Beckett

I sat next to Samuel Beckett
He didn't say a word
I didn't say a word
He said nothing
I said nothing
He had a pint of Guinness
I had a gill of whiskey
He read nothing
I read a script
I looked up
He lifted his glass to his lips
I think it was Beckett
His face looked like
an Ordinance Survey map
He cleared his throat once
I drank
He drank
shifted in his chair once
and it creaked
He didn't say a word
It must have been Beckett

¶ This book is set in the Thesis Sans family,
a typeface designed by Luc(as) de Groot in 1994.

acknowledgement[s]

I would like to thank the third cloud
on the left of the elm closest to the van,
the cloud that is unravelling, the elm
that twists in its own way.

Thanks also to the coffee house and bar
that provide tables for a small fee,
and to the ideological drugs I've
taken and the slow recovery from same.

Thanks to everyone who looks like
they do, and to the labyrinth of
the hawthorn, the garden, the
living room and the bedroom.

Thanks for my friends, who read
earlier drafts, though
the last draft is always best.

[PS. I thank all those who helped with these words:
from a Saskatoon Writer's Group, Anne Szumigalski,
John Clarke, David Carpenter, Dwayne Brenna; from
AU Press, Walter Hildebrandt, who asked for the
manuscript, and Pamela MacFarland Holway,
who fine tuned it. Ta.]

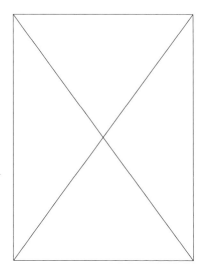

about the author

Max Frith is an author without
a single publication, no novel, no
book of poems, no play, but he has read
many books and attends movies
regularly. He has entered
many contests and writes at
odd moments in a school
scribbler. He won an eight-
minute poetry contest, and
pursues women at a
respectful distance.